CHILE

By Amy Holt and
Alicia Z. Klepeis

Published in 2025 by Cavendish Square Publishing, LLC
2544 Clinton Street, Buffalo, NY 14224

Second Edition

Website: cavendishsq.com

Library of Congress Cataloging-in-Publication Data

Names: Klepeis, Alicia, 1971- author. | Holt, Amy, author.
Title: Chile / Amy Holt and Alicia Z. Klepeis.
Description: Second edition. | Buffalo, NY : Cavendish Square Publishing, [2025] | Series: Exploring world cultures | Includes bibliographical references and index.
Identifiers: LCCN 2024022024 | ISBN 9781502672919 (library binding) | ISBN 9781502672902 (paperback) | ISBN 9781502672926 (ebook)
Subjects: LCSH: Chile--Juvenile literature.
Classification: LCC F3058.5 .K54 2025 | DDC 983--dc23/eng/20240808
LC record available at https://lccn.loc.gov/2024022024

Writers: Alicia Z. Klepeis; Amy Holt (second edition)
Editor: Jennifer Lombardo
Copyeditor: Jill Keppeler
Designer: Deanna Lepovich

The photographs in this book are used by permission and through the courtesy of: Cover xavierarnau/iStock.com; p. 4 Jose Luis Stephens/Shutterstock.com; p. 5 R.M. Nunes/Shutterstock.com; pp. 6, 14 reisegraf.ch/Shutterstock.com; p. 7 Dear Lady-Deer/Shutterstock.com; p. 8 Steven Sullivan/Shutterstock.com; p. 9 erlucho/Shutterstock.com; p. 10 Spectral-Design/Shutterstock.com; p. 11 Rumir/Shutterstock.com; p. 12 Andrzej Rostek/Shutterstock.com; p. 13 Nordroden/Shutterstock.com; p. 15 slowmotiongli/Shutterstock.com; p. 16 Raota/Shutterstock.com; p. 17 Pablo Rogat/Shutterstock.com; p. 18 The Photolibrary Wales/Alamy Stock Photo; p. 19 MARCELO DE LA TORRE/Alamy Stock Photo; p. 20 Aleksandar Todorovic/Shutterstock.com; p. 21 gonzagon/Shutterstock.com; p. 22 James Brunker/Alamy Stock Photo; p. 23 LOF Mapuche Kuruwinka 2 - Neuquén/Wikimedia Commons; p. 24 Esteban Garcia Pereira/Shutterstock.com; p. 25 ZemfiraS/Shutterstock.com; p. 26 imageBROKER.com GmbH & Co. KG/Alamy Stock Photo; p. 27 Philipp Edler/Shutterstock.com; p. 28 BearFotos/Shutterstock.com; p. 29 Larisa Blinova/Shutterstock.com.

CPSIA compliance information: Batch #CW25CSQ: For further information contact Cavendish Square Publishing LLC at 1-877-980-4450.

Printed in the United States of America

CONTENTS

INTRODUCTION

The country of Chile is a long, narrow strip of land on the west coast of South America. People have lived there for thousands of years. In the 1500s, Spain took control of the land. Chile won its independence in the early 1800s. Today, its government is a democracy.

People in Chile have many of the same kinds of jobs as people in other countries. Some work in banks or schools. Others have jobs in stores, hospitals, or offices. Many Chileans also work in mines, especially copper mines.

The capital city of Chile is Santiago.

Chile has many beautiful places to visit. There are deserts, beaches, and mountains. Tourists, or visitors, come from around the world to see the country's national parks and historic cities.

The Chilean people have many **traditions**. They value the arts. Dancing is popular here, and Chile is sometimes called the Land of Poets. Chileans also enjoy playing sports, especially soccer, and eating good food. Festivals and holidays take place all year long in this beautiful country.

Chile is home to many beautiful natural formations, including the Marble Caves (shown here).

GEOGRAPHY

Chile is bordered by the Pacific Ocean to the west, Peru to the north, Bolivia to the northeast, and Argentina to the east. The country covers about 291,930 square miles (756,096 square kilometers).

FACT!

Ojos del Salado is the tallest volcano above sea level in the world.

Ojos del Salado (far right) stands around 22,600 feet (6,888 meters) high.

The Andes Mountains run down Chile's eastern side. The highest point in the country is a dormant, or inactive, volcano called Ojos del Salado. A huge valley sits in central Chile. There are many farms here.

The Atacama Desert spreads across northern Chile. It is one of the driest places on Earth! Southern Chile, on the other hand, has a cool and damp **climate**.

This map shows where Chile is in South America.

THE DRAKE PASSAGE

To the south, Chile is bordered by the Drake Passage. This is a very deep waterway that connects the Pacific and Atlantic Oceans. The waters here are some of the roughest in the world.

HISTORY

A group called the Inca once controlled northern Chile. These Indigenous, or Native, people farmed and built roads to connect their cities. The Mapuche people, another Native group, lived in central and southern Chile.

FACT!

Many Chinese people moved to Chile in the early 1900s. They helped build a railroad system.

Chile controls Easter Island, which is in the Pacific Ocean. It is famous for these stone statues, which were made between 1400 and 1600 CE.

Starting around 1540 CE, Spanish **colonizers** took control of Chile. In the early 1800s, Chile fought a war with Spain for its independence. The fighting lasted for years, but Chile officially declared its independence in 1818. Things were shaky at first, but by the 1850s, Chile had gained political and **economic** security.

In 1973, a man named Augusto Pinochet led an overthrow of the government. He ruled Chile as a **dictator** until 1990. Although Chile is a democracy again, it has some human rights problems, such as police **brutality**.

Many places in Chile mark Independence Day with parades.

THE INCA EMPIRE

The Inca Empire covered all or part of the modern-day countries of Chile, Peru, Bolivia, Ecuador, Colombia, and Argentina. It was the largest Indigenous empire to ever exist in the Americas.

GOVERNMENT

Like many other democracies, Chile's government has three parts, or branches: legislative, judicial, and executive. Chile's legislative branch is called the National Congress. The National Congress writes new laws. It has two parts, which are called the Senate and the Chamber of Deputies.

The judicial branch is made up of courts. They decide whether the laws are fair, according to Chile's **constitution**. The constitution was put in place in 1980.

Although the capital of Chile is Santiago, the National Congress buildings and workers are in the city of Valparaiso.

Chile's first female president was Michelle Bachelet. She led the country from 2006 to 2010 and again from 2014 to 2018.

The executive branch includes the president and the cabinet of advisers. This branch enforces the laws, or makes sure people follow them. Chileans vote every four years for the president and the members of the National Congress.

FACT!

Chile's constitution was last updated in 2021.

A DEMOCRATIC REPUBLIC

Chile's official name is the Republic of Chile. A democratic republic is a type of government in which people vote for their leaders. Then, the leaders decide which laws will be passed and how they will be enforced.

THE ECONOMY

The amount and value of things a country produces is called its gross domestic product (GDP). Trade with other countries makes up about 75 percent of Chile's GDP. Its main trading partners are China, the United States, and Brazil.

Chile's money is called the peso.

A USEFUL CHEMICAL

In 2022, Chile was the world's largest importer of sulfuric acid. This chemical can be used to make many different things, including **fertilizer** for crops, car batteries, glue, and **dyes**.

The items a country sells are its exports, and the items it buys are its imports. Chile's main exports are copper and fish. It also exports fruit, wine, and nuts. The country's main imports are oil, gas, and cars.

The most common jobs in Chile are ones in which people serve others. These include jobs in stores, hotels, tour companies, and hospitals. People also work on farms and in factories.

FACT!

Chile is one of the world's largest exporters of grapes.

Copper can be used to make electrical wires, pipes, pots and pans, and much more.

THE ENVIRONMENT

Chile is home to many different animals. Alpacas and chinchillas live in the mountains. Pumas, pudu deer, and llamas live in forests and the plains of central Chile. Flamingos, penguins, and sea lions live along the coast.

Chile has some problems with its environment, or natural world. In February 2024, wildfires killed more than 100 people. Heat waves connected to climate change are making these fires worse.

The monkey puzzle tree, or Chile pine, is Chile's national tree. These trees are some of the oldest in the world.

Chinchillas can be found in Chile's Atacama Desert, which is the driest place on Earth. Chinchillas have adapted so well to this climate that they can get very sick if they get wet.

FACT!

In 2024, a group of Chilean **activists** bought the Cochamó Valley to save it from a land developer who wanted to build a power plant there.

Air pollution from cars and factories is a problem in Chile. Chile's government is working to help fight pollution and climate change. It has promised to get 70 percent of its energy from renewable sources such as water, wind, and sun by 2030.

FARMING FISH

Experts have raised concerns about the negative effects of Chile's salmon farms. If Chile does not change the way it runs its fish farms to be more environmentally friendly, there may be a worldwide shortage of salmon in the near future.

THE PEOPLE TODAY

Chile's population is about 19 million. About 60 percent of Chileans have a European background. Another 25 percent are a mixture of European and Indigenous **ethnicities**.

The Mapuche people make up about 9 percent of Chileans. In the past, the Mapuche were farmers. Today, some sell crafts or are involved in tourism. Many Mapuche live in the south-central part of Chile.

FACT!

About 1 percent of Chile's population is made up of multiple different Indigenous groups, including the Rapa Nui, Quechua, and Yagan.

A Mapuche woman spins wool to make yarn.

The Aymara make up another group in Chile. About 0.7 percent of the population is Aymara. Today, most Aymara people live and work in the coastal cities of Iquique and Arica. However, some herd llamas and sheep in northern Chile's high plains.

MAPUCHE BELIEFS

The Mapuche have a strong spiritual connection to the land they live on. In fact, their name means "people of the land." Many Mapuche care deeply about taking care of the environment.

These men and women are wearing traditional Chilean clothing.

LIFESTYLE

Most Chileans today live in cities and towns. Many have cell phones, computers, and cars. Some get around by taking the train or bus. Others bike or walk.

Some Chileans cannot afford to live in a city. Instead, they live in crowded areas just outside a city. These areas are called *campamentos*.

FACT!

It takes some Chilean children 2 hours to reach their school. They walk or ride the bus.

Homes in campamentos are small. Many people living there do not have electricity or running water.

Almost half the people working in Chile are women. Most work in service jobs, such as teaching and nursing. However, modern Chilean women are becoming doctors, judges, and more.

In Chile's countryside, most people work on farms or in mines. Along the coast, many Chileans work for fishing companies.

FAMILY TIES

Much of Chilean life is centered on the family. Family members help each other out and spend a lot of time together. Unlike men in many other Latin American countries, Chilean men tend to support their wives if these women work outside the home.

People who live in Chilean cities may go to the movies or play video games for fun. In the country, many activities are centered around farm life.

RELIGION

In Chile, people can practice whatever religion, or faith, they want—or no religion at all. Most people are Christian. About 42 percent are Roman Catholic, and about 16 percent are evangelical Christians.

Chilean Christians **celebrate** holidays such as Christmas and Easter. There are also festivals, or celebrations, for Catholic saints during the year. These sometimes include carrying religious statues through the streets.

FACT!
About 37 percent of Chileans say they follow no religion.

This giant Christmas tree sits in the Plaza de Armas in Santiago.

About 6 percent of Chileans follow other religions. The Mapuche have their own religious beliefs and traditions. Machi are Mapuche healers. People believe the machi can talk to spirits or gods. Some Mapuche combine their traditional religion with Christianity.

Shown here is a Mapuche religious **ceremony**.

AN IMPORTANT INSTRUMENT

An important part of the Mapuche religion is a type of drum called a *kultrung*. This drum represents the **universe**, which the Mapuche believe is divided into four parts.

LANGUAGE

Spanish is the most common spoken language in Chile. It is also the official language. This means it is the language the government and schools use. Many people speak Spanish for business matters.

Spanish is not the same everywhere in the world. It is not even the same everywhere in Chile! Different regions have different dialects, or ways of speaking the same language. Some words are different in Chile than they are in Spain.

FACT!
About 10 percent of Chileans speak English.

This sign in the Chilean city of Iquique is in both Spanish and English, and has a picture for people who cannot read either language.

This sign is written in Mapudungun. This language had no written form before the Spanish arrived in Chile.

Some Chileans speak more than one language. Many ethnic groups have their own languages. For example, many Mapuche people speak Mapudungun. Other Native languages include Aymara, Quechua, and Rapa Nui.

LOAN WORDS

Through travel and trade, people pick up words and customs from each other. Sometimes these loan words are changed to be more like the new language. For example, the Chilean word *cachay* comes from the English word "catch" and means, "Got it?"

ARTS AND FESTIVALS

Many Chileans value the arts. Painting and sculpture are common art forms. The Indigenous peoples of Chile create beautiful woven cloth and handmade baskets.

Dancing is an important part of Chilean **culture**. The cueca is Chile's national dance. Women perform it in colorful clothes. Men dress as cowboys.

FACT!
Many festivals in Chile are religious.

The charango is a traditional Chilean instrument. It is similar to a guitar, but it has 10 strings.

At some Chilean grape harvest festivals, people compete to see who can stomp grapes to create the most juice.

Chileans enjoy festivals all year. Some, such as Independence Day on September 18, are national holidays. On this day, there are parades and horse races. Children fly kites and play with spinning tops and marbles. Others are regional. The town of San Pedro de Atacama holds a week-long festival in June celebrating the saint its town is named for.

THE TAPATI FESTIVAL

Every February, the people who live on Easter Island have a festival to celebrate their culture. They paint their bodies, play music, dance, hold art and sports competitions, and tell very old stories.

FUN AND PLAY

Soccer, more commonly called football, is the most popular sport in Chile. The national team is very popular. Because the players wear red jerseys, fans often call the team *la roja*, or "the red one."

CHILEAN MUSEUMS

Santiago has many museums to visit. The Museum of Memory and Human Rights helps people remember the brutality of Pinochet's rule. The Interactive Knowledge Center includes three museums where visitors can touch and play with the exhibits.

Chile's national sport is rodeo. Rodeos came from the tradition of cowboys rounding up cattle.

Chileans and tourists often like to hike through the country. Patagonia is a popular area to explore. This region includes the Andes Mountains, grasslands, and deserts. Along the coast, Chileans like to sail and surf.

A game Chileans enjoy in the countryside is called *rayuela* or *tejo*. Players throw metal disks onto a plot of wet dirt. Points are awarded based on where the disks land.

FACT!

Chile has many hot springs for tourists and locals alike to enjoy.

The Atacama Desert is the perfect place to sandboard. People use snowboards to slide down the sand dunes.

FOOD

Corn and potatoes are common ingredients in Chilean cooking. *Humitas* are a quick meal. They are made of mashed corn that is wrapped in corn husks and cooked.

DESSERT

A tropical fruit called cherimoya grows in Chile. Chileans make a dessert called cherimoya alegre by combining pieces of the fruit with orange juice and sometimes a type of alcohol called Cointreau.

Fruits such as grapes, avocados, apples, and peaches grow in Chile. This worker is packing fresh peaches.

Because of Chile's long coastline, seafood is very popular. A cold dish called ceviche is typically made with raw fish or shellfish, lemon or lime juice, and seasonings such as cilantro, garlic, and red pepper.

When the weather is warm, people in Chile like to grill. An asado is a Chilean barbeque. Chileans grill steak, sausages, and ribs.

Chile's national dish is a stew called *cazuela de ave*. It includes chicken, corncobs, potatoes, and peppers.

FACT!

Many Chilean dishes blend Spanish-style cooking with local ingredients.

Cazuela can also be made with lamb or beef.

GLOSSARY

activist: A person who uses or supports strong actions to help make changes in government or society.

adapt: To change to suit conditions.

brutality: The act of treating someone with severe violence.

celebrate: To honor with special activities.

ceremony: An event to honor or celebrate something.

climate: The weather over a long period of time.

colonizer: A person who moves to a new place to live on land that was taken from Indigenous peoples.

constitution: A written document that outlines the laws of a country.

culture: The beliefs and ways of life of a group of people.

dictator: Someone who rules a country by force.

dye: A stain or color that is usually permanent.

economic: Relating to the way goods and services are made and sold.

ethnicity: A part of a person's identity based on where they or their family come from.

fertilizer: Something added to the soil that helps plants grow.

tradition: A long-practiced custom.

universe: Everything that exists.

FIND OUT MORE

Books

Anderson, Shannon. *Chile*. Minneapolis, MN: Bellwether Media, 2024.

Barghoorn, Linda. *Focus on Chile*. St. Catharines, ON: Crabtree Publishing, 2023.

Mather, Charis. *A Visit to Chile*. Minneapolis, MN: Bearport Publishing, 2023.

Websites

Kiddle: Chile Facts for Kids
kids.kiddle.co/Chile
Learn more interesting facts about Chile.

Kids World Travel Guide: Chile
www.kids-world-travel-guide.com/chile-facts.html
Read more about Chile, and take a look at some amazing pictures.

Video

Free School: Mysterious Moai
www.youtube.com/watch?v=QhEeh_BcADg
Learn more about the giant statues on Easter Island.

INDEX